A Note to Parents

DK READERS is a compelling program for beginning readers, designed in conjunction with leading literacy experts, including Dr. Linda Gambrell, Professor of Education at Clemson University. Dr. Gambrell has served as President of the National Reading Conference, the College Reading Association, and the International Reading Association.

Beautiful illustrations and superb full-color photographs combine with engaging, easy-to-read stories to offer a fresh approach to each subject in the series. Each DK READER is guaranteed to capture a child's interest while developing his or her reading skills, general knowledge, and love of reading.

The five levels of DK READERS are aimed at different reading abilities, enabling you to choose the books that are exactly right for your child:

Pre-level 1: Learning to read
Level 1: Beginning to read
Level 2: Beginning to read alone
Level 3: Reading alone
Level 4: Proficient readers

The "normal" age at which a child begins to read can be anywhere from three to eight years old. Adult participation through the lower levels is very helpful for providing encouragement, discussing storylines, and sounding out unfamiliar words.

No matter which level you select, you helping your read to learn!

LONDON, NEW YORK, MUNICH,
MELBOURNE, AND DELHI

For DK Publishing
Managing Art Editor Ron Stobbart
Managing Editor Catherine Saunders
Art Director Lisa Lanzarini
Publishing Manager Simon Beecroft
Category Publisher Alex Allan
Production Editor Marc Staples
Production Controller Rita Sinha
Reading Consultant Dr. Linda Gambrell

For Lucasfilm
Executive Editor J. W. Rinzler
Art Director Troy Alders
Keeper of the Holocron Leland Chee
Director of Publishing Carol Roeder

Designed and edited by Tall Tree Ltd
Designer Ed Simkins
Editor Jon Richards

First published in the United States in 2010
by DK Publishing
375 Hudson Street, New York, New York 10014

10 11 12 13 14 10 9 8 7 6 5 4 3 2 1

DK books are available at special discounts when purchased in bulk
for sales promotions, premiums, fund-raising, or educational use.
For details, contact:
DK Publishing Special Markets
375 Hudson Street
New York, New York 10014
SpecialSales@dk.com

A catalog record for this book is available
from the Library of Congress.

ISBN: 978-0-7566-6689-7 (paperback)
ISBN: 978-0-7566-6877-8 (hardcover)

Printed and bound in China by L.Rex
Discover more at:
www.dk.com

www.starwars.com

Contents

DK READERS

STAR WARS

THE CLONE WARS

Jedi Heroes

Written by Clare Hibbert

A galaxy at war

The Clone Wars are raging and the galaxy is divided. On one side is the Republic, led by Chancellor Palpatine and the Senate. In charge of the Republic's fighting forces is a team of Jedi heroes who lead loyal clone troopers into battle.

On the other side is the Separatist Alliance. Count Dooku leads it, but he reports to a secret, shadowy Master. Robots called battle droids serve as soldiers for the Separatists.

Guardians of good
The Jedi are a group of heroes who are sensitive to a mysterious energy called the Force. Led by the wise Yoda, the Jedi use the Force for good.

The role of the Jedi

In the past, Jedi Knights were able to defend the Republic, but they cannot cope with the Separatists. That is why the Republic needs clone troopers. It has created an enormous army with millions of these identical soldiers.

Galactic leader
The Republic is governed by a Senate, made up of elected representatives from all over the galaxy. The head of the Senate is Chancellor Palpatine.

The Jedi are still trying to bring peace and justice to every part of the galaxy.

They serve as generals in the Republic army, leading the clone troopers into battle. They also undertake solo missions to rescue hostages or to capture Separatist leaders.

Clone troopers take their orders from Jedi generals, such as Anakin Skywalker and Obi-Wan Kenobi.

The Jedi Council

The Jedi Council meets when there
are important decisions to be made.
Twelve of the best Jedi gather together
in the council chamber at the top of the
Jedi Temple. Those Jedi who cannot be
at the meeting appear as holograms.
Their leader is Grand Master Yoda.

Below the level of Grand Master is the rank of Jedi Master. To become a Master, a Knight has to perform heroic tasks or train a Padawan. Padawans are apprentices who are chosen from the younglings. These are infants who are sensitive to the Force and who join the Temple when they are very young.

Anakin uses the Force to lift Separatist general Lok Durd.

The Force

The Jedi's power comes from a
mysterious energy, known as the Force.
The Force has two sides to it—a light
side and a dark side. The Jedi heroes tap
into the light side of the Force and use it
for good. They protect and defend
innocent people and use the Force to
uphold the law of the Republic.

Those who use the dark side of the Force are called the Sith. They use the Force for evil, destroying things and forcing people to serve them. Count Dooku is a member of the Sith. He can turn the power of the Force into lightning, which he shoots from his fingers. During the Clone Wars, the Sith work under the leadership of a mysterious figure.

Count Dooku
The evil Count Dooku was once a Jedi Master, but he has now turned to the dark side of the Force. He commands the armies of the Separatist Alliance.

Jedi weapons

The lightsaber is a Jedi's weapon of choice. It has a blade made of pure energy and it can slice through almost anything. It takes a lot of practice and experience as well as a great deal of skill to control a lightsaber's powerful energy. Jedi train for many years to use a lightsaber correctly. A crystal in the lightsaber focuses its energy and determines its color. Obi-Wan Kenobi's lightsaber has a blue blade, Yoda's is green, and Mace Windu's is purple.

Yoda's lightsaber

Adi Gallia's lightsaber

Jedi can use lightsabers for many things, as well as for fighting.
For example, lightsabers are very useful when slicing through a locked door.
The Sith also use lightsabers.
Some can use two lightsabers at once, others use a double-bladed saberstaff.

The evil assassin Asajj Ventress uses two lightsabers which she can join together to make a saberstaff.

Grand Master

Yoda is the Grand Master of the Jedi Order. He may be small in size and ancient in years, but the Separatists are afraid of this Jedi hero.

Yoda duels and defeats many enemies, including Count Dooku. He can also outsmart whole squadrons of battle droids single-handedly.

After centuries as a Jedi Master, Yoda is extremely sensitive to ripples or disturbances in the Force. He can sense the exact whereabouts of other Jedi anywhere in the galaxy, and he knows when they are in danger.

Even though he is very old, Yoda can slice his way through an army of battle droids.

Expert negotiator

General Obi-Wan Kenobi is a strong
swordsman, but fighting isn't his first
choice when it comes to problem-
solving. This hero prefers to use words,
not weapons. After talking to Obi-Wan,
enemy commanders often surrender
rather than fight. Master Kenobi also
offers advice to his former Padawan,
Anakin Skywalker—though
he doesn't always follow it!

Captain Rex

Rex is a tough, experienced clone trooper captain. His unit, the 501st Legion, serves under Anakin. Rex fights alongside Skywalker and Obi-Wan in many key battles.

Obi-Wan distracts General Loathsom so that Anakin can complete a mission during the Battle of Christophsis.

Impetuous Knight

Born on the planet Tatooine, Anakin
Skywalker is sensitive to the Force,
but is not always true to the Jedi code.
Jedi should not form overly emotional
links with others, but Anakin does.

Padawan training

Padawans are taught by a Jedi Knight. Anakin's Padawan is Ahsoka Tano. Training a Padawan is one way a Jedi Knight can become a Jedi Master.

Anakin duels Count Dooku among the sand dunes of Tatooine, Anakin's home planet.

When Skywalker fights, he is fearless but sometimes reckless. Yoda hopes that training a Padawan might make Anakin more responsible.

Brave Padawan

Ahsoka Tano is a Togruta, a species
from the planet Shili. She first meets
Anakin during the Battle of Christophsis.
Anakin worries that Ahsoka will slow
him down, but he soon recognizes the
great bravery and talent of his Padawan.

Ahsoka's bravery can lead her into
danger. She is a little rebellious and
sometimes has trouble following orders.

*Ahsoka discusses plans with
Anakin and Obi-Wan.*

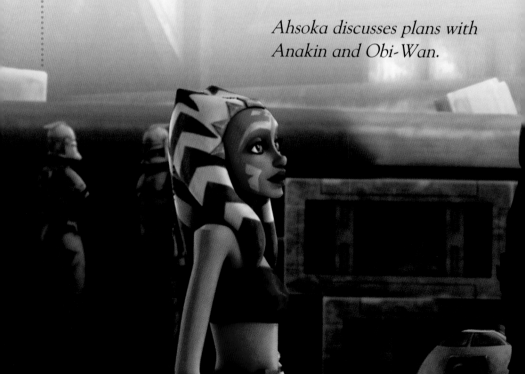

Babysitting
Rotta is the son of Jabba the Hutt. When Rotta is kidnapped, Ahsoka and Anakin have to rescue him and return him to Jabba.

Ahsoka has a softer side, as well. She shows this by caring for the sick baby, Rotta the Huttlet. Of course, she is very loyal to Anakin.

Tough taskmaster

Luminara Unduli is a Jedi Master from
the planet Mirial. All Mirialans are
agile, but Luminara's tough training has
made her even more flexible. She is also
incredibly acrobatic and very skilled
with a lightsaber.

> **Ventress**
> Asajj Ventress works for Dooku and the dark side of the Force. She hates all Jedi, but especially Obi-Wan and Anakin.

Luminara's abilities with a lightsaber make her a fearsome Jedi hero.

Despite her skills, Unduli almost meets her downfall at the hands of Asajj Ventress. The assassin nearly defeats the Jedi while she is on her way to Coruscant, the Republic capital. Luckily, Ahsoka comes to Unduli's rescue, and the two Jedi force Ventress off their ship.

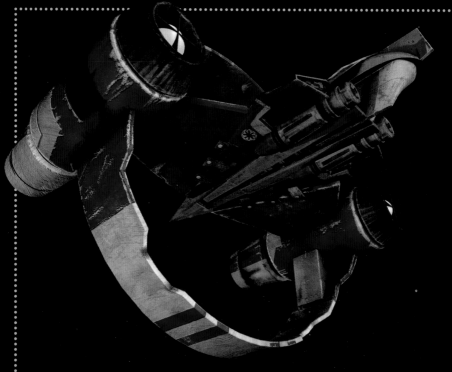

*Jedi starfighters need to attach to a
special ring to jump into hyperspace.*

Ships for heroes

The Republic fleet has many ships and
the largest are Jedi cruisers. They have
16 turbolaser turrets and can provide
unrivaled firepower.

Attack shuttles are the usual
transport for VIPs and diplomats, while
Jedi generals prefer to fly starfighters.

Anakin flies his starfighter into battle against the Separatist fleet.

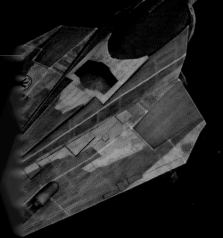

The Twilight *might look old, but it can outrun anything.*

As well as his starfighter, Anakin flies a battered old freighter called *Twilight*. He has modified the clunky old ship to make it fast and agile.

Hyperspace jumps
Spaceships travel faster than light by taking a shortcut through hyperspace. Stars zoom by during the jump.

Frontline hero

Mace Windu is one of the best Jedi swordsmen and is also renowned for his wisdom. He rose to the top of the Jedi Council, and became Master of the Order. However, he gave up this role at the beginning of the Clone Wars.

This allows him to see action on the frontline, leading troops into battle.

Windu takes part in the first Battle of Geonosis. He also commands the mission to free the Twi'leks on Ryloth when their planet is under siege. During the Ryloth mission, he has to use his negotiating skills. He persuades the Twi'lek freedom fighter Cham Syndulla to help capture the city of Lessu.

No battle droid is a match for this Jedi hero and his lightsaber.

Expert pilot

Plo Koon comes from the planet Dorin, which has little oxygen. He can survive in space—for short periods, at least. This proves useful when his cruiser is destroyed by the Separatist battle cruiser *Malevolence*. He has to fight battle droids that attack his escape pod.

Plo Koon controls a starfighter as if it is his own body.

Plo Koon is a very brave and highly skilled pilot. He has led a squadron of Republic fighters heroically during many space battles.

Discovering Ahsoka

Plo Koon discovered Ahsoka when she was just a baby. Seeing she was sensitive to the Force, he sent her to be brought up as a youngling in the Jedi Temple.

Nautolan Jedi Master

Master Kit Fisto was trained by Yoda and is a valued member of the Jedi Council. He is a Nautolan and can detect tiny changes in body chemistry with his tentacles. He uses these to "read" how people are feeling.

Count Dooku lures Fisto and his former Padawan, Nahdar Vebb, to General Grievous's castle on one of the planet Vassek's moons. Fisto needs all of his lightsaber skills to battle Grievous, and he very nearly defeats him.

Scary cyborg
General Grievous is a cyborg—mostly robot and a little bit living being. He is trained to use a lightsaber and fights with four at the same time.

The new Knight

Nahdar Vebb is a Mon Calamari with big, bulging eyes. He is the former Padawan of Jedi Master Kit Fisto and has only just become a Jedi Knight. Vebb is keen to fight the Separatists and eagerly accepts any mission he is offered. He is happy when he joins Fisto in tracking down the escaped Separatist prisoner Nute Gunray.

However, they have been lured into a trap at the lair of General Grievous. Inside Grievous's fortress, they have to fight a monstrous roggwart. They kill the roggwart before facing General Grievous himself. Vebb has to battle the cyborg on his own when the two Jedi are separated, with disastrous results.

Grievous tricks Vebb and kills him with a hidden blaster.

Veteran and mentor

Master Aayla Secura is a Rutian Twi'lek and one of the Jedi Order's bravest and most skilled generals. She is respected by her fellow Jedi: Padawans look up to her as a mentor.

Secura connects more strongly with the Force by meditating.

Secura has spent many years developing her combat skills. She is an expert with a lightsaber and has faced powerful foes, including Asajj Ventress.

Among the many battles Secura has fought is the defense of Maridun. Along with Anakin Skywalker and Ahsoka Tano, she helps a tribe of peace-loving Lurmen defeat a Separatist force who want to try out a deadly new weapon.

Skilled warrior

Adi Gallia is a Tholothian and a courageous member of the Jedi Council. Thanks to her contacts, the Jedi find out that Nute Gunray is stirring up trouble on the outskirts of the galaxy.

also a skilled warrior and
...obi owes her his life.
...ir mission to rescue Jedi Eeth
...a steps in just as Grievous is
...ll Obi-Wan. Her skill with a
...ends the cyborg running!

Nute Gunray
Viceroy Gunray
is a Neimoidian
and a leader
of the Trade
Federation.
He plots to
kidnap Senator
Padmé on the
planet Rodia,
but his plan is
foiled and he
is captured.

Model Padawan

Barriss Offee is everything a trainee Jedi should be—responsible, brave, and respectful. When she forms a partnership with Ahsoka Tano, Luminara Unduli fears that Ahsoka's rebellious streak might affect Barriss. Unduli need not have worried. Offee and Tano bring out the best in each other. Their daring mission to blow up a Separatist weapons factory on Geonosis is a success.

Brain worms
For a brief time, Barriss is infected by a brain worm when it crawls inside her head. This beast takes over her brain and turns Barriss against Ahsoka. Ahsoka's only hope is to freeze out the worm.

Separatist hunter

Jedi Master Eeth Koth has an important role to play during the Clone Wars. His mission? To hunt out Separatists. He spends his time leading a task force tracking down enemies of the Republic in the Outer Rim of the galaxy.

It takes a squad of commando droids to capture Koth.

Grievous plans to use Koth as bait to lure more Jedi into a trap.

Unfortunately, Grievous ambushes Koth's cruiser and commando droids take the Jedi prisoner. The Separatist general tortures Koth, but Grievous has forgotten that Eeth Koth is a Zabrak. Like all Zabrak, he has supreme mental strength and can withstand great pain. He stays strong, even when Grievous is electrocuting him.

Instinctive Jedi

Jedi Master Ki-Adi-Mundi is a Cerean and a member of the Jedi Council. He is an expert swordsman and can use the Force to create powerful blasts.

Mundi takes part in both battles on Geonosis and the hunt for Poggle the Lesser, who is selling droids to the Separatists. During the second battle, he and his troops are shot down and crash far from friendly forces. How will they join the others in battle? Mundi uses his Jedi powers to show him the correct way to join up with Obi-Wan and Anakin. His instinct guides the Jedi and leads him through a cave through the Geonosis cliffside.

*Mundi was taught by
Grand Master Yoda.*

Elderly Jedi Master

Tera Sinube is an elderly Jedi Master who has a detailed knowledge of the criminals on Coruscant. This wise Jedi embarks on fewer and fewer missions as he ages. He is very excited, therefore, when Ahsoka Tano asks him for help in tracking down her stolen lightsaber.

Sinube soon shows that he is not as frail as he looks. His knowledge helps them to find the thieves and he has a trick up his sleeve when it comes to a fight. His walking stick hides a lightsaber which he can wield with great agility.

Chief librarian
Ahsoka is advised to speak to Sinube by chief librarian Jocasta Nu. Nu is in charge of the Jedi Archives, which hold thousands of years of Jedi knowledge.

Future heroes

Padmé Amidala may not be a Jedi, but she is brave, good, and dedicated to the Republic. She represents her home planet of Naboo in the Senate.

At the beginning of the Clone Wars, Padmé secretly marries Anakin, even though Jedi are not supposed to form permanent attachments. Padmé's secret love for Anakin will change the course of galactic history. In the future, the fate of the galaxy will depend on their two children, Luke and Leia.

Loyal "Jedi"
He may be clumsy, but Jar Jar Binks is Padmé's trusted friend. When the Senator is betrayed on Rodia, Jar Jar sets out to rescue her— disguised in a Jedi cloak!

Glossary

battle droid
A soldier robot. Most of the Separatist army is made up of battle droids, also known as "clankers."

clone trooper
A soldier created to serve in the Republic army. All clone troopers are genetically identical.

Clone Wars
A troubled time in galactic history when Republic forces fought Separatists.

Coruscant
The capital of the Republic, this planet is home to the Senate, Jedi Temple, and Jedi Council Chamber.

cyborg
A being that is partly a living organism and partly a robot.

electrocute
To give someone powerful electric shocks.

the Force
The energy that flows through all living things.

hologram
A 3-D image of someone or something, made of beams of laser light.

hyperspace
A region through which spacecraft pass when traveling faster than light.

Jedi Knight
A member of the Jedi Order who has studied as a Padawan under a Jedi Master and who has passed the Jedi trials.

Jedi Master
A rank for Jedi Knights who have performed an exceptional deed or serve on the Jedi Council.

lair
Another word for a "hideout." General Grievous's lair is on one of the planet Vassek's moons.

lightsaber
A swordlike weapon. A lightsaber has a blade of pure energy, and is used by Jedi and Sith warriors.

mentor
Someone who other people learn from and look up to.

Padawan
A youngling who is chosen to serve an apprenticeship with a Jedi Knight or Master.

saberstaff
A special lightsaber with two blades instead of one, used by the Sith.

Senate
The government of the Republic, with representatives from all parts of the galaxy.

Separatist
Against the Republic; belonging to the Confederacy of Independent Systems.

the Sith
Warriors who, like the Jedi, are sensitive to the Force, but who use its dark side.

youngling
A Force-sensitive child, who is trained in the Jedi Temple and may one day be a Padawan.